W9-AGB-947

SIDEBROW BOOKS

sped

Published by Sidebrow Books
P.O. Box 170113
San Francisco, CA 94117-0113
sidebrow@sidebrow.net
www.sidebrow.net

Cover art by Augustine Kofie
Cover & book design by Jason Snyder

ISBN: 0-9814975-7-8
ISBN-13: 978-0-9814975-7-0

FIRST EDITION | FIRST PRINTING
9 8 7 6 5 4 3 2 1
SIDEBROW BOOKS 008
PRINTED IN THE UNITED STATES

Sidebrow Books titles are distributed by
Small Press Distribution

Titles are available directly from Sidebrow at
www.sidebrow.net/books

A Member of

Sidebrow is a member of the Intersection Incubator, a program of
Intersection for the Arts (www.theintersection.org) providing fiscal
sponsorship, incubation, and consulting for artists. Contributions
to Sidebrow are tax-deductible to the extent allowed by law.

TERESA K. MILLER

sped

SIDEBROW BOOKS + 2013 + SAN FRANCISCO

ACKNOWLEDGMENTS

Many thanks to the editors of the journals in which excerpts from *sped* first appeared or were reprinted: *Coconut, Diagram, slouch, E*ratio, Moria, Kadar Koli,* and *Cricket Online Review.*

Tarpaulin Sky Press first published "Forever No Lo" as a chapbook in November 2008.

In memory of Marvin Gene Miller, 1948 – 2006,
and for Gregory, who showed me how much is still here

In time of peace what children feel concerns the lives of children as children but in time of war there is a mingling there is not children's lives and grown up lives there is just lives and so quite naturally you have to know what children feel.

—Gertrude Stein, *Wars I Have Seen*

Forever No Lo

I had to turn away from Jesus/ a pouring forth captured in wood/ carved blood spilling from every rib, every limb// On CNN World Edition the school children of Darfur hold up fingers representing the number of relatives killed/ two, three, five, six/ mother, two sisters/ mother and brother/ father// *Não quero nada, obrigada*// Armfuls of abalone bracelets and small giraffes shaped by pocket knives/ *Italiana? Alemã? Portuguesa? Americana?*/ The merchant smiles/ bows and says Presents from Africa//

A senhora fale inglês? Sabe onde fica o Bosch?// In a rare traveling exhibit/ the Polish allow him to hang on a wall in Iberia/ two floors below the freestanding triptych screen/ color on one side, black and white on the other/ mental file next to the two-inch-square monochrome from World History// Meg Hamill wrote about a one like every other one, every dead one, and outside was the hummingbird tree/ a whole tree chittering with hummingbirds on the oval// He is gray/ the blood worn but nauseating//

The children hold up their fingers and make lists:/ mother and father/ three sisters/ father// A luxury to see the religion as morbid, obsessed with dying/ Mary Jane says people must identify with the suffering// Imagine losing the cat second only to losing my father, much easier would be losing my partner// The train left Macondo filled with bodies from the marketplace/ the train that brought the gringos and their scales to weigh bananas// The thorns dig into his grained face// *Pai*//

I have no fistula, not thinning hair, no pulmonary scar tissue from chemotherapy// The woman on the *linha azul* taps her white cane against the floor, the legs of standing passengers/ wails something blending together// *Escreva?*// She writes imagined death notices, all those birds outside/ and don't you see that the things we named paved the road to forever no more/ as much as the thorned evenings smoldering on the couch?/ The overnaming to thicken a veneer too much for the points to punch through//

Não é nada// Dear X, I might be in love with you/ no matter the extra ten years trailing behind/ your first kiss before I had the chance to emerge from the spinal/ wide eyed/ and grab my father's beard// Every hand in the classroom raised, and I hold one finger to the television// Iraq Body Count to differentiate the victims from one and one/ from third deadliest month in war// Her cane clicks against the standing pole/ one eye a red gouge, one never emerged/ one eyelash stuck to smooth skin stretched over a sphere/ no opening//

In crime/ in encouraging the worst in each/ in the summer heat along the world's largest ocean or on the largest freshwater dunes// I said Where is your purse, she said Right here, I said Where is your purse, she said It was right here// *mala sem alça*/ We are not in Brazil, thank you// Imagine what your penis looks like, what your beer gut looks like under your too small T-shirt// Dear X, I think I am in love// Not a tumor larger than my back, no tapeworms, not an eye without access to the light//

He brings *couverts*/ a spiral of shrimp heads/ green
and black olives/ *pão e queijo*// Madam, would you
believe me if I told you they were professionals?/
But she said Where is your purse, and I said
Right here// *Não quero nada, obrigada*/ *Tem o café
americano?*// At the dinner table he dissected the
banana, examined it under a magnifying glass,
weighed it/ Prelude to the massacre, to the years
of rain/ blame the train that brought the gringos//
How do you expect to sell anything when *não fale
inglês?*//

Would that you would introduce a mode whereby I would not have to spend forty-eight hours pretending I haven't read your note/ reply as if I could be doing something else// His skin was not white as it now appears in every picture, in carved Polish trees/ hanging in Lusitania// The fisherman's sunburned eyes surrounded by dark cork skin/ hands effortless maneuvering the twin screw, *duas gringas* and a Kodak// Praia Dona Ana/ There is the small elephant/ There is the big elephant//

No photos please, OK?// In the ossuary neat stacks of bones/ femurs on femurs, skulls perched on top// How can we hate the rain the gringos brought/ the banana company and the massacre/ when we are gringos bringing our own rain, refusing *couverts*?// On CNN World Edition the woman who survived the church massacre sweeps the dust and leaves from around the piled bones/ the memorial/ Hutu widow of a murdered Tutsi//
Aqui você tem dois euros, muito obrigado//

In the ossuary the dusty nobles dream of water in the Moorish cistern// On BBC the men arrive at the *Gacaca* singing in the back of a barred pickup// Easiest because I could replace her with a new addiction/ Dear X// I had to turn away/ her cane clicking against the polished shoes of rush-hour commuters/ the blended words, the crowd pushing to separate// Because God knows which legs supported which torso carried which skull// We always come to Lagos now/ It's the quality of life//

Today I know there will be forever no Lo, and the women around me know too// *O embaixadade?//* It forgives in this deepest place those moments I kept for myself before I had to tell you our afternoons added up to nothing you could hold// *Desculpe, o senhor sabe onde fica a embaixada?//* All of the papers that should have been in the money belt, *os euros,* your passport// On every channel they are searching for Madeleine/ There is an inflatable billboard now//

We are an ignorant people, but I do know where Washington is/ No, no, I didn't mean// No Lo and every low/ What about the times when all assembled discuss in detail the preparations of their dead relatives' bodies/ the embalmed aunt shipped from Tanzania/ the unscattered ashes living in the towel cupboard/ where on the Olympic Peninsula they'd like to go should something, you know// In Lagos color fliers on every door/ Taken from Praia da Luz/ a speck in her eye// We wait *na estaçao*//

You have the ugliest president in the world// What
if I told you you could hold now/ that I hope you'll
have waited// My finger to the television screen in
a quiet corner of my brain// And you know what
are the worst, funeral home services/ they feel so—
empty// *o monumento para os pescadores perdidos*//
I needed to get that money I inherited but she
wouldn't take care of it/ It's like, that has nothing
to do with your dead mom, it's just getting your shit
done// We peer in the window just as a live lobster
flops to the floor and writhes on the tile//

So that no one would go in search of the cars filled with bodies/ no one would question the story// That is a good Catholic name/ You are so beautiful/ God must smile on me today// Here is a story I remember: Girl 1 says, Do you have a cat?/ Girl 2 says, No/ Girl 1 says, Do you have a dog?/ Girl 2 says, No/ Girl 1 says, Do you have a—/ Girl 3 says, You know she can't have pets in the shelter// *Na estufa* the doves are alone, one to a caged grotto// *Sim, a embaixada, perdão*//

My mother could just barely do a French braid/
sent me to school puffy headed to play with the little
girls in tight plaits/ Mothers quilting/ No relatives
fresh from prison// I dreamt your beer gut was
a smooth concave stomach, ran my fingers along
your waistband/ You said almost/ What if I have
crossed myself into *uma mulher perdida*// I would
have invited you to my birthday, but my mom says
you live too far away// *a criança perdida*// They sing
and stomp the ground and defend their neighbors
and accuse them//

On the train to Faro we sit with an English horticulturalist who keeps saying *cheers* and *brilliant/* scans for a conductor when I eat bread and cheese in my seat// And what if a man who was like your brother but was not did become the Zahir/ What if we both saw it// *S'il ne marche pas, je peux revenir, et vous pouvez m'assister, n'est-ce pas?*// Once you start talking, you can't stop the tape until it's finished// She touched his skin and said Lordy!// Along the waistband, convex or concave//

The lowest point after seven hits of Ecstasy/ cut with heroin/ three bottles of water/ blowing into the ashtray and watching the cloud settle on my shirt/ *Picture of Dorian Gray* moment in the bathroom, waiting for you to wonder where I'd gone for so long and come rescue me// Fog moving from the palace *ao castelo mourisco*, where we cling to the walls// The trail of blood ran out the door and across town and Ursula screamed and they could not contain the smell of gun powder//

The town I've planned for us is in the East Bay in the Northwest/ six sunny days for every rainy one/ and the colder days are still clear/ You study in your too tight T-shirts/ *e a mulher foi encontrada*// He tells us they strip the bark every nine years/ Underneath the tree is not brown and weathered like *pescador* skin but black// The Italian tourist captures the Megalithic phallus from every angle/ Not a Kodak but a Nikon// Did you ever truly believe in lesbians by trauma?//

He tells us they feed *as bolotas aos porcos* and that's why they taste so good, the pigs// Imagine this is as far as you sing alone/ One day I write you a letter and you don't wait to respond// They turned the megalith into *a igreja*/ long gray stones extended back into a room/ stuccoed/ painted white and blue/ filled with pictures of dead soldiers, candles painted with The Virgin/ spiders working inward from the dank corners// We needed to choose a container in which to cremate the body//

A virgem, in a way/ Are you a man who thinks like that?// Here is a story I remember: We saw a roman candle shoot over the hemlocks toward Alki, and the child turned to me and asked Is that like an IED?// She said they ranged from $90 to $2,000// They sing in the barred truck and the lawyers speak into microphones and the women stand in front of their community/ He dragged my sister onto the road and beat her unconscious in front of my two nephews// I said The $90 one/ He never would have burned up $2,000//

The blood made of wood hangs overhead/ The blood made of blood runs from the severed leg/ It was an improvised explosive device/ It was an American bomb// *Quanto custa?*// She said So you want the plywood box with the cardboard lid// There are five ways into hell, three in color// Madam, you see we deal with so many of these—illegals—these—aliens// He was in India on a headset/ Did you do anything nice for Father's Day?// Where is your passport?// *Sou de Marrocos*//

Quanto custa, esta guerra?// She did not come into the bathroom/ I did not leave/ I couldn't remember how to pee// Yes, he is the ugliest/ That's why we came here// What does that mean, *in love with*, anyway?// No thank you, no presents from Africa// Roughly translated, she said Coffee! American! Excuse me! Thank you! Please!// We took the small pile of burned bones in a bronze book/ put them behind glass where they could dream of water// When she used to draw a black X on each hand//

I believe them when they say In a beautiful place
out in the country// No house would get more
shade than any other/ by the swamp// A room
in Lisbon to hang our collective anguish// They
could not escape/ The car ricocheted/ A highway
on one side, a wall of blackberry vines// The ones
like every other one/ separate ones// Now X
contemplating father, partnered, curled around cat/
The one remembering the hummingbird tree//
mais baixo// Imagines the broken skull blood//
And what of the hand that carves and paints the
thorns//

The Apiary

It started with a few bees going where they needed to go by walking on the ground// In our low-context culture, disability exists biologically within the individual// I called her again to say her son was making throat noises/ refusing to stay in his seat// We went to the movies and sat in a row of friends not holding hands and he said I'm going to be a dad// The mind clamps down on all the sounds outside/ nighttime morning birds/ another oversize motorcycle broadcasting R&B// A cable snapped and the cars snaked for miles//

So much dependence on a sentence/ clause as unit of meaning// Then they turned up on their backs, legs crawling in the air/ or crouched in a ball on the ground and stopped moving// You remembered him as the air being filled with birds/ Versus full of// She told me he was becoming a young man, finding his place in the world/ Yes, but he said Excuse you// A collection of tiny earthquakes that trace a fault line/ Inexorably, the bottom of the ocean// Disability is both reified and in need of fixing//

They stopped moving, the bodies clustered by the elevator, a few on the stairs// It is not contextual/ not in relation to society or duty or what is expected of an individual// What is your fatherhood in relation to a nuclear family severed from context// *We will never begin again*// Always discovering bacteria that live in the dark// Here is what I want you to bring on your honeymoon/ She fucked me and the light was too bright through the door// We fucked and there were bright lights// The boiling/ a mile underground//

We choose which is worse/ cold or lack of natural light/ If we grow toward warmth or the window// Until we were poised to enter into that particular contract, it still appeared a network/ a million branching tributaries flowing backward to points of possibility// A shiny brown cocoon/ smooth and pointed at one end/ packed with cotton in a glass jar because that's what keeps things safe// This is where you say Are you a political animal/ bifurcated, transformed, or exposed/ Which part of you is what you always were/ A sentient animal narrates reversal as return/ to avoid shame//

He is defiant and what will you do about it that I cannot// They were squished a few at a time/ constellation of crushed exoskeletons// Who is she as you pass this small body back and forth, if not yours// His shrunken five-foot frame no longer pulling itself up by the handrail// Time to remove the insides and sell the shell// It rose like a cargo plane/ a dirge for the papered-over window/ the crack of light we earn by the cold// You get to say whatever you want, and say it, and say it, and say it//

There grew something more than the line, than a book about prosody you gave me for graduating from high school// We will never almost sleep again/ click of the rice cooker through the doorless basement apartment// A chair could earn a C if it sat quietly all year// Before them were the bats/ hanging dead in caves/ white fungus growing from their nostrils// I told her Disability must be fixed if this is the only life we have, and if we live again, it will be fixed then// If we began as horsetails or crabgrass in the cleft of a rock/ were earthworms and juncos, organisms in deep sea trenches// She said Thank you for calling//

What lets you write the canon of loss// A drawer of
screws and loose paperclips/ Full as opposed to filled
with// 92% of us carry around plastic estrogen//
Pathways through his catacombs/ a honeycomb/
center of every compartment an unexpected//
The state tells me they need to understand integer
operations// What is he, and whether that makes
him spoken for// Sitting on his lap was the perfect
antidote whether you meant to or not//

How long before you can no longer stand your own
company// Didn't not, double negative/ It's the
same as adding a positive// There are doubts during
a dry spell/ A diamond ring in a nutcup wrapped
in a greasy paper napkin// Before the bats wasps
under the eaves/ nothing to make for us, paper and
bites/ masks and poison spray, a vacuum cleaner
for the strays// There was a backup plan that went
pregnant/ that became suddenly unappealing//
An actual biological fact tethered in the body//

Twelve shoeboxes filled with paper collars from new dress shirts// Every neon windbreaker coming up the hill was you/ I could pull over and offer to take you home/ suggest you prefer the exercise before dinner/ think you back into existence// Hold your minus forearms up and show me how it works/ cross them into a plus// We know a disability because we cannot fix it/ because it lets us make do but will not abate// I have seen some on the wall above the stairwell, just clinging// Out of context it is one body sleeping//

We will never drive again/ drunk dozing carload from 2am Milwaukee// Disability has precise cognitive measurements and discrepancy thresholds// We are just so proud of him, whatever you've been doing is working// He looks at your breasts, and sees you see him looking, and you still have to make conversation for the rest of the grocery store line// A plastic bag inside a box packed with plastic bags/ and inside it a zippered pouch/ holding crumpled tissues/ wrapped around six rotted teeth with gold fillings//

Where is their hive and why did you settle for mechanized translation as intentional language// We were no less careful than I have been with anyone else// An exhibition/ real video of car crash victims// The desire to be born works its way back and spills over the rim of the condom// Seven pairs of new blue slippers and one used/ matted/ worn through// The freeway grew deafening through the window/ unsaleable, unabideable// There is something to two bodies in a room, working in parallel// If through carelessness I could remake you//

There are never two close enough to crouch together// We walked from Union Square to Lombard to get the ring for the wedding I knew wouldn't happen// Emotional disturbance is disproportionate, overly reactive/ irrational behavior without any other explanation// Every car accelerating/ every semi, chains rattling/ someone else has to get there right then// Black and white photographs of children we do not recognize with dogs// We cannot locate it, but disability must exist within the individual//

Promise me you will always want me and never die//
Bought the two-pack on sale/ inferred sympathy
behind the clerk's blinking shadowed lids// She
weighed almost nothing/ hadn't learned to bend at
the waist to sit on my lap// He tried to push one
out of harm's way with his shoe but crumpled it on
its head// My mother said Why they didn't get rid
of her I have no idea/ It's only a bundle of cells at
that point// The pollen mixes in, and you eat the
thing you're allergic to, and it cures you//

The idea begins to crystallize after it sits a while/ Return to find an overgrowth in the empty spaces// Months or years later, the jar wrapped in a handkerchief at the bottom of a box of treasures that weren't// Cotton laced with brown powder, a dead moth pressed against the glass// I opened the package on the walk home/ went into the bathroom while you slept/ drops of urine on the sink// Never again// Sound of the too small air conditioner/ home to a hatching nest of spiders// Waited to count the lines//

I remembered them motionless on the second and third floor landings// If your head were broken and the division fell out/ memory, sounds into words, sights into numbers/ attention a collage of impressions stripped from context// Bodies smeared from wings collecting on the stairs to the garage// Incense dust blowing off the windowsill and all over the desk/ I said Oh, do you live upstairs and he said I own this place// And if they get to our cars will we drive them away/ Escape or renunciation, my life to relive the black box tapes// Refugees came but we could only transcribe/ gestational diabetes, post-traumatic stress/ the exact moment she coughed tuberculosis into my mouth//

Almost fifteen and in eighth grade and everywhere strumming a ukulele/ We must hold a determination meeting to document whether his behavior is a manifestation of his disability, which is a physical fact in his neurobiology// Behind every bookshelf another fat black spider wielding front legs like hooks// She said We have been having the same dream/ the one where you yell louder/ and the kids fall more apart// I was sure I could feel myself becoming a milk machine/ a school driver/ a look at my son not quite doing what I never quite did//

They are so still you can pet the fuzz, but they shudder// I turned the desk on the slant to roll toward it instead of away/ only the corner of the corkboard stayed on the wall// Portuguese acres of gnarled brown trees/ bark peeled off in wide black rings// In every storefront a church and a man who wants to walk me home to my boyfriend because my skin is so soft// Except there is no cure, only desperate offerings/ oxygen therapy, elimination diet, blood transfusion, chelation// We speak in tongues, writhe on the ground/ broken headed//

Opened the fire escape and quiet multitudes of translucent green flies assembled on the ceiling// The things we hold on to/ a series of chambers built up room to room/ we will finish by fire, dumpster, abandon// Each of his words you swallowed/ brought its own punishment// Threadbare swagger and eye contact two beats too long/ the illusion of seeing, of being seen now clear and hollow// Breach birth, failure to progress, lead in the paint, mercury in the water, infant meningitis, traumatic brain injury// She told me to close my eyes and imagine it's the sound of the ocean/ but it's the opposite of the ocean//

We learned to use people-first language/ My description is not that you are a myopic person// The 11-year-old in diapers crawls under the desks, saliva-soaked white T-shirt clenched firmly in his jaw// It is good that she makes eye contact, worrisome that she will not crawl// We gathered them into paste with wet paper towels/ green streaks overhead// He is with autism/ Every day the sprinklers outside cause an unmanageable behavior degeneration//

She is in a sling between us, a thing you use to pass her back and forth// What we can't undo/ can't do over/ will never do again// The threshold would or would not marry/ a barstool, a baby's head and otherwise swaddling// If we were once a stream of words at the bottom of the ocean/ A biological fact finds its place// The exoskeleton cracks/ They are made of something that stains// What is the head but a skull when blunt force spills the life out/ red against your green windbreaker//

Programs for Exceptional

Spring came/ a spiraled wire// I've said this before/
before the panel/ was summarily Chaucered//
Life came of the broken thing/ the fracturing//
What no one will admit in the terrorism porn
industry/ in the ever/ returning questions// What
did he look like there in the grass/ I wasn't there/
Yes, but how do you feel he must have looked//
and the tenderness I feel/ will send the dark underneath//
Left the gathering children who matter for the
children of tuberculosis// Clapping and swaying/
I am a promise// They know how to say it better
than we do/ I do not miss you/ gave up asking
vestmented strangers your destination// It is you
who are// *Tu me manques//*

If asked Do you know what a black hole is?/ you would say/ ← → // In the new horizontal the fall runs on loop/ the projector crackling with tiny imperfections/ waiting to spread across the film// The birthday girl asks Can I dance on stage with you?/ already gyrating in a cut-off miniskirt// We perceive the crackling as the sound of the flickering/ as thunder the sound of lightning// We tell each other the caught phrases/ *N'importe quoi!*// First bell at 8:53/ 4-minute passing period// Sure, can I wear your tiara?// You sang the soundtrack all the way to Los Angeles// Imagine the engine revving//

A, Yes/ I can't explain it// Ben Lerner sees the error of cognition in conflation/ *the event and the event of the event's image/* the towers falling and the clip of the towers falling/ staggered across all major networks// In the new horizontal, you are my projection onto the space you occupy on stage// I cannot help but be blunt, I am so very German/ I am here to convince you to work in Moderate/ Severe// Or B, No/ I can't explain it// The strength of your fingers on the strings// *Ils ont survécu à une guerre*// If given the choice/ would you get back in the car/ shattered windshield and rims ground into the pavement/ try to drive away// And if you are missing from me/ where does that leave//

We are in harnesses coming off the bus/ We are runners// Democracy means/ ← → // A paper placeholder for attachment we lost track of/ before we replaced each other// An error of cognition to conflate the event of the car I never saw veering onto the bike path, throwing you onto the windshield, with the event of my imagining the event/ repeated on loop/ crackling// You know this expression?/ *les sans-abri*?// Hand cradling the neck/ feet working the pedals// It's like your genetic code throws an exception// A featureless body in the center of the screen/ stripping the layers away//

Watching the lights change from red back to green/
How old are you today/ 21// We are humming/
We are humming/ Folding our ears forward/
humming/ thumbs tucked inside// Math and
scientific theory whose texture you like/ your
sensibility seduced by nomenclature/ by accolades
for your cross-genre genius// Unopened stacks
of bank statements chronicling your drowning//
Her father passes me the blunt/ explains the word
for rat's tail/ slang for penis/ *Ils sont les mêmes*//
The falling and the wire// I think we're all a little
Aspy// Fingers light on the keys/ monotone/ 21/
can you believe it//

This is Moderate/Severe// For instance, black holes have no hair/ Explain that to me// I stopped noticing if she came to bed// So it begins// He gives the critic an out/ forgiveness/ tacit permission to assign value to the event of the event's image, its accuracy of capture// *En France*, we do not eat the bread the second day// In love with twin names/ The one abusing prescriptions/ shamed into hours searching for details on indie boys with guitars/ The one who used to play guitar/ snort crank/ fuck unprotected// Humming/ programmatic// He told me he fell in the only patch of soft grass/ I felt something brightly green/ but then I went/ saw the garbage//

The fall captured on film/ in text/ tapestry//
A new you limps in/ crunchy with an earring/
coming from a common country// We are
humming/ Humming// His fingers begin to twitch
in his lap/ suddenly fly toward his face, full flexion
and extension/ rapid anxious climb// *Obsolète est
aussi l'allumeuse*// For instance, the equivalence of
matter and energy/ Draw me a diagram// This is
the exception, the outlier// And all to win a street
race/ No, I can't imagine// You see she is in the
second percentile// Miniskirt and combat boots/
swept up and the close bodies chanting/ *She told
me not to fuck with straight girls/ She told me not to
take pills*//

Pornographic in its insistence/ cutting to action/ ten angles on repeat// We are not allowed to say that in the hole where the yous are missing/ something new grows// Architect unrolls plans for a new sort of coupling/ a blank space where it is not the voice of strangers but the voice of// We attribute this to/ ← → // Ashamed to build something new/ disrespect your memory// Yes, I have prostituted/ but if the money goes toward the Revolution// *Oui, c'est une contradiction, je sais*// Afraid not to grow back/ squander your memory// *Just because you feel it/ doesn't mean it's there*// So if the car broke through nothing/ if you fell onto scraggle-grassed litter//

For instance, the reason the stars are not evenly distributed/ and whether we are expanding away from the center/ like a bullet or a body on a bungee cord/ infinitely or about to snap back to nothing// What color is the bus, Jackie?/ - / Is the bus yellow?/ - / Say Yellow/ Say—// And Will Oldham crackles over a spare acoustic/ When you have no one/ no one can hurt you// So it begins// I said in my best/ *Je prends d'eau/* like Homer Simpson/ and he spat-laughed in my *potage//* Eugene deciduous/ that miniskirt again// What about letting him make you a straight girl// We are tracing hand over hand/ and all the children are left behind//

The broken amp tube and a whole history in the audience/ Your tattooed fingers, a baby kicking toward the monitor// His attempt to share his premonitory dreams started the crack, into which the wedge/ And what if I told you I saw this coming too// Louis, you're going to burn in hell somewhere/ No, that's from the heart// Is that correct classroom behavior?// In front of the class/ the exchange/ I have a job after school/ *Sur la rue!/ Je peux comprendre*// The expansion to instantly/ to ever available// The algorithm/ program assigning a standard score to your aptitude/ your taste// We told them not to try him as an adult//

Bungees back to compact/ to local// In the new horizontal/ everywhere I go/ Someone jokes about SUVs running over bicyclists/ The garbage truck dragging the guy on the fixie// Double Dare Ya/ This tattoo sits on a timeline you began with a mixtape ten years ago// The event of the event's image is reduced/ dusty primary colors/ the background fuzzy/ radiating out from basal fractures of the skull// My image of you pressing me against your car/ one of my legs around your waist// A stranger calls from Belgium/ interrupting dinner/ Our exchange student explains It is for to talk with a man about sex/ but she is not, how do you say/ *sérieuse*//

Vous seriez fier d'elle, écoutez// Danny, sit down/
Danny, sit down/ Sit down/ Sit please/ Danny, sit
down/ Sit down/ Sit down please/ Thank you/
- / - / - / Danny, sit down, sit down// What you
really chased after, the same as his freighter trip to
St. Vincent/ car abandoned in a Manhattan alley/
Not a body as flint but an alternate ending// The
fate you don't know over the one you dreamt//
cf. valentine/ If your girlfriend made love to you
in every room of the house/ twice a day/ for five
days/ would you/ ← → // A bar full of L.A. hair
metal// She was wearing a shirt and no pants/
I know/ that's the style//

I was counting particulate matter samples from city air/ entering them into Excel sheets/ as your fingers ran up and down those plastic keys// Do you remember that night—which night—you got so drunk/ held the microphone in your cleavage/ wouldn't stop singing over and over again/ Papa was a rodeo// Like he was counting six-pointed snowflake variations/ The Book of Sand// She welded a tree together in the basement soon to be a flood// The exceptional children/ on the spectrum// *De l'eau, pardon*// Radiating out from blunt force injury to the head// The roots had nothing left to hold/ and it fell downstream//

Or perhaps he merely accustomed himself to it, so it was
not the pain that diminished but his attention to it//
Lerner says we often name things after the manner
in which we destroy them// How many Madrases
at Café du Nord/ close talking about NYC/ our
eyes on the cradling of the neck// Your set broke
my mind// Why did you get kicked out of class?/
Teacher said something about F's, and this girl
she's all That's Gerard's grade, so I'm like That's
yo mama's grade, so she kicked me out// What
do you think you should do next time?// A plane
flies 300 land miles per hour/ Janice travels 1,750
miles/ How many hours does it take?//

What do you do next?/ I don't know/ 3 goes into 5 how many times/ 1/ multiply/ subtract/ drop it down// He woke in the night and screamed and grabbed her ankle/ Father sending the sleepwalker away as a rapist// I spent the first Easter xeroxing death certificates/ Blunt force injury// *les sans-coeur*// Spring comes after winter/ What season comes after winter? Spring/ What season comes after winter?/ - // We scan the program/ count the remaining verses// Trade your Thunderbird for a stint clearing trails/ he'll never walk again// But there's a remainder/ What do we do with remainders?/ Here/ we put them here//

Jackie/ Jackie/ Say spring/ - / Say spring/ - //
Your multiple choice/ to stay// At least he didn't
have to live like a Christopher Reeve// The
silhouette of a body/ flapping its wings/ an angel
made of lead// *I knew something was missing*// The
clip falling/ repeating// Out our window we watch
the docent march tourists up to the cupola and
wave across the lawn/ another exhibit// A book is
portable/ but filled with burned bones// She said
Do you want to hold it/ set the weight of you in
my arms/ against my chest// *Just take me everywhere
you go*// Read the sentences silently to yourself and
tell me a word that fits in the blank// *Un jour au
printemps le corps du père* _____ //

For instance, I had imagined a low wall along the highway/ not by the blackberry vines but by the road itself/ She told me it was there// I spent the whole month before your arrival forwarding the CD to 1:36/ listening to you sing I'll beg a little/ on repeat/ plaintive/ crackling// David took the dinghy past the edge of the reef/ shattered it on the waves in the night/ returned on a piece of driftwood// The event of imagining a car breaking through an imaginary wall// She hisses the esses in *laissez*/ frowns at my voiced *z* sound// But she caused the fall/ her arrogance/ not to leave knowledge// Could have been well enough alone//

Sí? That's Spanish/ No, it is yes/ in response to a negative question// Here is a story I remember: The girl was classified nonverbal, had been caught masturbating in the severe autism class, would not follow directions/ One day I heard her singing to herself on the monkey bars/ in Vietnamese// You took me to see Sleater-Kinney at RKCNDY/ Carrie brushed her hand on my thigh/ making her way through the crowd// *Even in the midst of grief the mind grapples with a hundred impressions: a pain below the heart/ an odor on the breeze//* Your daughter travels at a standard score of 67/ Would you// ← → //

Alright, Boolean expert// The event itself is not an image/ cannot be repeated// Your new horizontal is splayed in the grass/ is a plywood box fed to the incinerator// *Society did this to you/ Does society have justice for you?*// Think of it as a Rubik's cube/ not a collection of random pieces// What of repetition with slight variation// Next time throw yourself off the bike and into the blackberry vines// The fall on loop/ sealing our fate// He said I was *une prostituée*/ Next time call him *con*// The exceptionally what/ That's the euphemism// Yes, it is a contradiction, I know// The body that grew from the missing/ wishing for your return// *If/ not/ I/ do/*/

[*To the tune of Wagner's "Bridal Chorus"*]: Go fuck yourself/ Go fuck yourself/ Stop treating me like one of the retarded kids// Things were easier the first time around/ more narrative, maybe// I woke/ mess of sweaty hair against my face/ realized you've been channeling Russell Edson all along// When she got off the bus, the girl jumped her/ And I had to call the police to tell them the events that perspired// The vertical falls to the new vertical// The wirewalker gets to the 104th floor dressed as a construction worker/ lies on a line between the north and south towers// *les sans-securité*// One leg wrapped around the boundary/ the women and the pavement rising to make him unrecognizable//

His multiple choices// Because I only liked to play Barbies when I could cut off their hair/ color it with Sharpie/ or make them ask each other math questions whose answers you didn't know// Less free association/ more colored squares shifting// You should know I've become the you who made me the me who left you/ only with someone/ - // Padding around the apartment/ approaching paralysis/ the radiator clank// *All my love was down/ in a frozen ground*// A, To speed past the semi// Can you tell me what a word means/ Just do your best/ Does this affect my grade/ Just do your best// Or B, To let it go// *On ne voit qu'avec* _____ // If rightly one could only//

Maybe if my breath/ firm enough against my own mortality/ against yours// Barbie parks her pink Corvette/ tiptoes to the chalkboard/ Is this an example of the associative or commutative property of multiplication?// *Un jour le cycliste* _____ *sur son vélo*// And in paralysis/ a fire escape// Some time ago this all looked so good on paper// Spring cleaning your shirts and shoes to Goodwill// *If I lived forever you just wouldn't be so*// ← → // Here is a story I remember: The blond boy pulled down his jeans, urinated on the astroturf in a one-handed plank position/ Everyone gasped/ The teacher said Don't cry, tell me about Lee Harvey Oswald again//

It is standardized/ There are no exceptions// She wants to tell me about restorative justice// My students flashing gang signs/ pretend sniper fire out the window/ picking off second graders in PE, one by one// My samples were long strips of tape looped on the windowsill/ and I counted the pieces that stuck// The photograph of the memory we share/ a rumpled paper Sharpied/ NO MORE DUST MASKS// The smell of what we cannot name/ burning in the concrete/ particles blowing uptown on the breeze// *On ne voit qu'avec ceux qui ont perdu*// And the soundtrack a patriotic march/ beneath the stars and stripes/ strung between the brownstones// Who are we//

And if you are missing from me/ when does that leave// If I must give up where you are/ where do I// They forgive first/ grieve after// *Oh father let's go down in the river*// The body of Christ/ the blood of// After the fall/ we collected the pieces left/ played the sample on loop// I have no video recording/ no voice// The Tutsi mother told the murderer You must come to my house every week so I can feed you as my son/ you have taken from me// When you leave your body/ ← → // Just the fading memory repetition// Radiating out from lacerations of the brain// The blood of/ kept inside/ so the grass stays scraggle-green// Where do we put the remainders?// Here// We put them here//

NOTES

// *Forever No Lo*

Nods to Gabriel García Márquez's *One Hundred Years of Solitude*; Meg Hamill's *Death Notices*; Jorge Luis Borges's "El Zahir"; Boards of Canada's "In a Beautiful Place Out in the Country"; iraqbodycount.org; a number of international news reports seen or overheard in a smattering of hotels and flats; the beautiful continental Portuguese language, transcribed here primarily as butchered, not as used by fluent speakers; and the Museu Nacional de Arte Antiga

// *The Apiary*

Kalyanpur & Harry's *Culture in Special Education* and Joanna Klink's "Sorting"

// Programs for Exceptional

Portishead's "The Rip"; Susan Raymond's *I Am a Promise: The Children of Stanton Elementary School*; Ben Lerner's *Angle of Yaw*; James Marsh's *Man on Wire*; Stephen Hawking's *A Brief History of Time*; MC Solaar's "Obsolète"; Team Dresch's "Uncle Phranc"; Jean-Luc Godard's *La Chinoise*; Radiohead's "There There"; Palace Brothers' "You Will Miss Me When I Burn"; Anthony Doerr's *About Grace*; Bikini Kill's "Double Dare Ya"; The Magnetic Fields' "Papa Was a Rodeo"; Jorge Luis Borges's "El libro de arena"; Lamb's "Gold"; 20 Minute Loop's "Book of J"; 7 Year Bitch's "M.I.A."; Bon Iver's "Re: Stacks"; Antoine de Saint-Exupéry's *Le Petit Prince*; and Goldfrapp's "Pilots"

Teresa K. Miller grew up in Seattle. She lived in New York, received her MFA from Mills College, and taught college English in Chicago before becoming a special education teacher in the East Bay. This book owes much to lessons from students.

SIDEBROW BOOKS | www.sidebrow.net

SIDEBROW 01 ANTHOLOGY

A multi-threaded, collaborative
narrative featuring work by 65 writers

SB001 | ISBN: 0-9814975-0-0

NONE OF THIS IS REAL

Miranda Mellis

SB005 | ISBN: 0-9814975-4-3

ON WONDERLAND
& WASTE

Sandy Florian

Collages by Alexis Anne Mackenzie

SB002 | ISBN: 0-9814975-1-9

WHITE HORSE

A collaborative narrative featuring
poetry and prose by 25 writers

SB006 | ISBN: 0-9814975-5-1

SELENOGRAPHY

Joshua Marie Wilkinson

Polaroids by Tim Rutili

SB003 | ISBN: 0-9814975-2-7

LETTERS TO
KELLY CLARKSON

Julia Bloch

SB007 | ISBN: 0-9814975-6-X

CITY

Featuring work from The City Project

SB004 | ISBN: 0-9814975-3-5

BEYOND THIS POINT
ARE MONSTERS

Roxanne Carter

SB009 | ISBN: 0-9814975-8-6

To order, and to view information on new and forthcoming titles,
visit www.sidebrow.net/books.